I'm in Charge of What?
Walking in Stewardship

Book Nine
Walking with Jesus
Becoming the Best Me I Can Be

Pamela D White

All scripture quotations, unless otherwise indicated, are taken from the Holy Bible, **New King James Version©**. Copyright © 1982 by Thomas Nelson, Inc. Used by permission. All rights reserved.

Scripture quotations marked NIV are taken from the Holy Bible, **New International Version** ®, NIV ®. Copyright © 1973, 1978, 1984 by **Biblica, Inc.® Used by permission. All rights reserved worldwide.**

Scripture quotations marked NASB are taken from the Holy Bible, **New American Standard Bible®,** Copyright © 1960, 1971, 1977, 1995, 2020 by The Lockman Foundation. All rights reserved.

Scripture quotations marked AMP are taken from the Holy Bible, **Amplified**, copyright © 2015 by The Lockman Foundation, La Habra, CA 90631. All rights reserved. For Permission To Quote information visit http://www.lockman.org/

Scripture quotations marked ESV are taken from the ESV® Bible (The Holy Bible, **English Standard Version**®). ESV® Text Edition: 2016. Copyright © 2001 by Crossway, a publishing ministry of Good News Publishers. The ESV® text has been reproduced in cooperation with and by permission of Good News Publishers. Unauthorized reproduction of this publication is prohibited. All rights reserved.

Scripture quotations marked NLT are taken from the Holy Bible, **New Living Translation,** copyright © 1996, 2004, 2015 by Tyndale House Foundation. Used by permission of Tyndale House Publishers, Inc., Carol Stream, Illinois 60188. All rights reserved.

Scripture quotations marked MSG are taken from **THE MESSAGE**, copyright © 1993, 2002, 2018 by Eugene H. Peterson. Used by permission of NavPress. All rights reserved. Represented by Tyndale House Publishers, Inc.

Scripture quotations marked AKJV are taken from the Holy Bible, **Authorized King James Version**, The Authorized (King James) Version of the Bible ('the KJV'), the rights in which are vested in the Crown in the United Kingdom, is reproduced here by permission of the Crown's patentee, Cambridge University Press. The Cambridge KJV text, including paragraphing, is reproduced here by permission of Cambridge University Press.

A publication of Blooming Desert Ministries

ISBN 978-1-7370803-6-7 (sc print)
ISBN 978-1-7370803-7-4 (ebook)

Printed in the United States of America
Copyright © 2021 by Pamela D White
All Rights Reserved.

IngramSparks Publishing (Ingram: Lightning Source, LLC)

One Ingram Blvd., La Vergne, TN 37086

Publishing Note: Publishing style capitalizes certain pronouns in Scriptures that refer to the Father, Son, and Holy Spirit, and may differ from other publishing styles. **All emphasis in the Scriptures' quotations is the authors.** The name satan and related names are not capitalized as the author's preference not to acknowledge him, even though it violates grammatical rules.

No part of this book may be reproduced or transmitted in any form or by any means, electronic or mechanical – including photocopying, recording, or by any information storage and retrieval system – without permission in writing from the publisher. Please direct inquires to PDW Publications.

Dedication

This book series is dedicated to you.

Everyone has opportunities to become a better version of themselves. My prayer is that this book series helps you on that journey. The Lord loves you so much He desires an intimate relationship with you. You are special to Him and He loves spending time with you. Walking and talking with Jesus every day should be the norm, not the exception. Life can bring difficult circumstances and situations. When you walk with Jesus, life events, are not only manageable but can be turned for your good.

"And we know that all things work together for good to those who love God, to those who are the called according to His purpose," Romans 8:28.

Come with me into this exploration of how you can develop a relationship with Jesus and walk with Him every day. This is an opportunity to become a better you.

Acknowledgments

The Great Commission given by our Lord and Savior Jesus Christ noted in Matthew 28:16-20 is my inspiration for this publication. Verses 19-20 state, *"Go therefore and make disciples of all the nations, baptizing them in the name of the Father and of the Son and of the Holy Spirit, teaching them to observe all things that I have commanded you; and lo, I am with you always, even to the end of the age."* This verse is the very basis for missionary work all over the globe. I have been blessed to be able to serve in a few of those missions. Missions are an amazing experience. I came to realize though that everyone cannot always do all the parts commanded in these verses. I can't always go. I didn't often get to baptize. What I realized was that I can do my part in teaching to observes the truths of the Scriptures. My desire to fulfill the teaching part of the Great Commission was the inspiration for this work. My pastor, Bishop Larry Taylor, and First Lady Desetra Taylor allowed our church to use these Bible studies in our New Life Discipleship classes for nearly twenty years. The work has also been used in prison ministries in central Illinois for as many years. The teaching has proven effective in changing many lives and discipling the children of God. Thank you, Bishop and First Lady, for teaching a balanced spiritual and natural life so I could complete this project and see the impact of the work on people's lives.

Bishop positioned me to be the director of New Life Ministries Discipleship for several years. New Life classes were designed to teach those new to Christianity or new to the church the foundational truths needed to build a solid life in Christ. During that time, this work was fine-tuned with the help and input from the dedicated, gifted, and anointed New Life teachers Minister Retta Smith, Minister James Smith, Minister Debby Henkel, Dr. Terry Husband, Minister Char-Michelle McDowell, Minister Yvonne Smith, Minister Herbert Smyer, and Professor Susan Gibson along with the encouragement and guidance of Dr. Chequita Brown and community service advocate Minister Patricia Turner. I also want to give a shout-out to Dr. Wanda Turner, nationally acclaimed minister, teacher, prophet, life coach, mentor, and best-selling author, who continued to encourage me to just publish the thing! Thanks to all of you. Each of you has made a significant impact on my life.

My dear friend and mentor, First Lady Marshell Wickware, supported the project and pushed me to publish it for years. Thanks for not giving up on me!

My life-long friend, Robin McClallen, thank you for all your support, input, and encouraging me to publish something. You have been instrumental in making me an author.

A special thanks to my husband, Brian K. White, for his patience and prayers as I spent hours and hours researching, writing, and rewriting. Thanks, BW!

Most of all thank you to the Holy Spirit and my Lord and Savior Jesus Christ. I present this work in obedience and honor to You.

Contents

Introduction	11
Definition of Steward	13
Definition of Christian Steward	13
Stewardship Opportunities	17
Stewardship of Time	17
Stewardship of Abilities/Gifts	19
Stewardship of Relationships	20
Stewardship of our Physical Bodies	21
Stewardship of the Environment	23
Stewardship of Possessions/Money	25
Kingdom Economics	27
Stewardship of the Tithe	27
Stewardship of the Offering	31
Stewardship of Saving	32
Stewardship of Investing	33
Stewardship of Budgeting	35
Overflow Principle	37
Stepping Stones	41
I'm in Charge of What?	43
Glossary	45
About the Author	51

Book Nine

I'm in Charge of What?
Walking in Stewardship

OBJECTIVE

As a Christian, you carry many titles. One of those titles is 'steward' and the job of a steward is to practice stewardship. This lesson presents the importance of Christian stewardship, what stewardship means, and how to practice stewardship.

MEMORY VERSE

"For by him were all things created, that are in heaven, and that are in earth, visible and invisible, whether they be thrones, or dominions, or principalities, or powers: all things were created by him, and for him," Colossians 1:16 KJV.

I'm in Charge of What?
Walking in Stewardship

A. Walking in Stewardship
 1. Definition of a Steward
 2. Definition of a Christian Steward

B. Stewardship Opportunities
 1. Time
 2. Abilities/Gifts
 3. Relationships
 4. Physical Bodies
 5. Environment
 6. Possessions/money

C. Kingdom Economics
 1. Tithe
 2. Offering
 3. Saving
 4. Investing
 5. Budgeting

D. Overflow Principle
 Living in God's abundant provision

I'm in Charge of What? Walking in Stewardship Introduction

To understand how to be a Christian steward and to practice Christian stewardship, it is important to understand what a steward is and whose things you are stewarding. The best way to understand stewardship is to go back to Genesis. Genesis 1:1, the very first words in the Bible, spell it out clearly. *"In the beginning God made the heavens and the earth."*

Let's do a little Bible review with that verse.

When: In the Beginning

Who: God

What: Made the heavens and the earth

Where: In the middle of chaos (Genesis 1:2)

Why: Good question. God is extremely complex and yet ironically, God keeps it simple for you and provides some insight within the Scriptures. Isaiah 6:3 tells you the earth is full of His glory. Psalm 19:1 says the heavens declare the glory of God. So I think it's safe to say that heaven and earth were created to shout out the glory of God. He also created heaven and earth for fun. God enjoys His creation. Psalms 104:31 says the Lord rejoices in His works. Genesis 1 tells you over and over that as God created, He was very pleased and called what He created good. The amazing news is that when God made all these wonderful things, He created man (Adam and Eve) in His image and then blessed them by giving them dominion over all the earth. God made this magnificent, beautiful creation and then gave it to humans to enjoy.

Understanding stewardship begins with a realization that everything is **from God, for God, and belongs to God**. Everything is God's. Then the Lord does an amazing thing. He entrusts you, the one made in His image, to watch over all of creation. God trusts you to keep good stewardship over His gift to you. God gave you everything that was given so you could give Him glory and for both His and your enjoyment.

Definition of Steward

A steward handles the affairs of others. It is the steward who acts as an agent for the owner and actively directs affairs. In ancient kingdoms, stewards ran countries when the king was away and were required to be prepared to give a full account of their actions upon the king's return. They act in place of the king! That is a lot of power. When the king was present, the steward handled daily affairs. A steward carries a great deal of responsibility and must always be prepared to give an account for their decisions and actions regarding that which they were governing.

Definition of Christian Steward

Christian stewardship is the same as the dictionary definition of steward, except the one who gave you stewardship is the greatest and mightiest King ever. Stewardship began when God entrusted the earth to Adam and Eve. God placed creation in the hands of the first family and gave them the privilege of dominion over creation and the blessing to continue fruitfulness, multiplication, and dominion.

"Then God said, "Let Us make man in Our image, according to Our likeness; let them have dominion over the fish of the sea, over the birds of the air,

and over the cattle, over all the earth and over every creeping thing that creeps on the earth." So God created man in His own image; in the image of God He created him; male and female He created them. Then God blessed them, and God said to them, "Be fruitful and multiply; fill the earth and subdue it; have dominion over the fish of the sea, over the birds of the air, and over every living thing that moves on the earth" Genesis 1:26-28.

Not only does the Lord give you an entire world to enjoy and rule, but he gives you rewards when you take good care of it. Luke 19:11-27 tells the parable of a nobleman who went to a far country and left his kingdom in the hands of ten of his servants to steward in his absence. Some used their portion to multiply and increase just as God had told Adam and Eve to do. Others had done nothing with their entrusted portion. When the master asked for an account and found out some had done nothing, he called it wickedness. Then he took away from those who did nothing with their portion and the 'do-nothingers' were considered enemies and slain. Wisdom would say when God entrusts something to you, be fruitful and multiply it to your fullest ability and reap the rewards.

You don't want to become confused that anything is yours. Psalm 24:1 says, *"The earth is the Lord's and all its fullness, the world and those who dwell therein."* The New Testament confirms that in 1 Corinthians 10:26, *"For the earth is the Lord's, and all its fullness."* That is everything. The earth —the blue ball—countries, territories, districts, regions, tribal land, inhabitants, the underworld, cities, ground, space, air, water, the moon, everything. Its fullness—its entire content, everything on it from the highest mountain to the smallest microbe. The world—everywhere that is inhabited and not inhabited. Those who dwell therein—every single living thing.

Everything!

Did you get it yet? Everything is God's. Everything. Have you ever created something? A craft, a painting, a poem, a book, a model airplane, a detailed Lego Star Wars Millennium Falcon? Didn't it feel great when you were done? Did you feel proud and want to display it so everyone could see it? I still have things my kids created when they were young. They may have forgotten them by now, but they were so proud of them at the time that I can't bear to toss them and some of them are still on display.

God created all things. John 1:1-3 says, *"In the beginning was the Word, and the Word was with God, and the Word was God. He was in the beginning with God. All things were made through Him, and without Him nothing was made that was made."* No matter how high, how low, visible or invisible – God created it. *"For by him were all things created, that are in heaven, and that are in earth, visible and invisible, whether they be thrones, or dominions, or principalities, or powers: all things were created by him, and for him,"* Colossians 1:16 KJV. His creation pleased Him so much that He wanted to share it with someone, so He made you and entrusted this amazing creation to you.

Now you know. God made everything. What are you supposed to do with it? As a mature Christian steward, your job is to be responsible and dependable to walk in obedience to the commands and will of God. He said be fruitful and multiply; have dominion; be faithful. 1 Corinthians 4:2 spells it out pretty well. *"Moreover, it is required in stewards that a man be found faithful"* KJV. Also, don't complain, but have an attitude of gratitude. When you recognize everything is God's and you are the caretaker, then you can be thankful for all God has created and for His generous gift to you. And most importantly, remember that God's gift of creation is for His glory and honor. Let Him know you appreciate it as John did in Revelation 4:11 by speaking words of praise, *"You are worthy, O Lord, to receive glory and honor and power; for You created all things, and by Your will they exist and were created."* Show Him gratefulness by obeying Colossians 3:17 *"And whatsoever ye do in word or deed, do all in the name of the Lord Jesus, giving thanks to God and the Father by him"* KJV.

Stewardship Opportunities

Now don't get overwhelmed or fearful of the responsibility you have as a steward of the Lord. God will not give you more than you can handle, and He will equip you to care for everything in your part of the world. You know that your mailbox and the TV can be full of opportunities to save whales and rainforests and pleas to feed the hungry, keep water clean, stop littering, and hundreds of other opportunities. Maybe you are a person called to help with one of these causes. Maybe not. You certainly can't do it all, but you can take care of what God entrusted to you and anything the Lord leads you to support. Pray for God's direction on how to take care of what is in your circle of influence. God has delegated a variety of things to you to steward. Here are a few of the things that have been assigned to your stewardship.

STEWARDSHIP OF TIME

Your time in this life is short compared to eternity. It is also a gift to use to its full potential. Ephesians 5:15-17 reminds us, *"Be very careful, then, how you live—not as unwise but as wise, making the most of every opportunity, because the days are evil. Therefore do not be foolish, but un-*

derstand what the Lord's will is" NIV. Does this mean you can't sit and watch TV, and you have to work all the time? OF COURSE NOT! Take a vacation, read a book, watch your favorite TV show, but keep balance in your life. There is **A TIME TO WORK AND A TIME TO REST**. Manage your time wisely and ask God how to best use your time. A common complaint is that there are not enough hours in a day. That is a sign that you are not using your time wisely. If you needed more hours, God would have given them to you. When you give your days, hours, minutes, and seconds to God and ask for His help in utilizing the time you have, He will show you how to get rid of things that are clogging up your minutes and distracting you from what you should be doing. He will show you how to use the time you have to spend time with Him, accomplish what needs to be done, and still have time to rest. He will take the time you have and multiply it supernaturally.

Remember, time is a created thing. Eternity has no time. That is why 1,000 years can be like a day and why the Lord can see your past, present, and future all at one time. The fourth day of creation was when time was created and the sun, moon, and stars were put in place to govern time. *"Then God said, "Let there be lights in the firmament of the heavens to divide the day from the night; and let them be for signs and seasons, and for days and years,"* Genesis 1:14. Because time is a created thing, in Christ you have dominion to rule it. The key to time stewardship begins with seeking Him first. When you take time to center your life around the Lord, things just fall into place and time isn't a problem anymore. Then maybe set a timer on your phone so you don't forget your kid at soccer practice!

"But seek first the kingdom of God and His righteousness, and all these things shall be added to you," Matthew 6:33.

STEWARDSHIP OF ABILITIES/GIFTS

God has given you talents and gifts to accomplish your purpose in life and to bless others. Because of sin-nature, it's hard not to be a self-aholic. There are a couple of traps that attempt to snare you as a self-aholic. One is that you think too highly of yourself. You become full of pride in your gifts and abilities. You think you can do things better than anyone else. Your pride can also go in another direction. You can develop a prideful false humility and feel that you aren't good enough, that you don't have what it takes, and you don't have any gifts or abilities of any worth. You may feel that others don't give you enough appreciation and acknowledgment. These attitudes rob you of fully developing and using your gifts and abilities for others. You are to be a good steward of your gifts. God gave them to you through His grace. You don't deserve them, but in His love, He gave them to you, anyway. The Lord wants to bless you through your gifts, and He wants to bless others through your gifts. Your gifts are special and unique to you. To be a good steward of your gifts, ask God how to develop them, and then do it. Take some lessons or classes or find a mentor to guide you. Your gifts are for serving the body of Christ, encouraging and edifying each other, and giving glory to God. The highest calling is for you to be exactly who God called you to be. Be the best you that you can. The 'you' that God created has a specific purpose. The fallenness of this world will attempt to give you a false identity, so your purpose is not fulfilled and your gifts and abilities are unused. Find the real you and develop that person. You are the best gift.

"As each one has received a special gift, employ it in serving one another as good stewards of the manifold grace of God. Whoever speaks, is to do so as one

who is speaking the utterances of God; whoever serves is to do so as one who is serving by the strength, which God supplies; so that in all things God may be glorified through Jesus Christ, to whom belongs the glory and dominion forever and ever. Amen," 1 Peter 4:10-11 NASB.

STEWARDSHIP OF RELATIONSHIPS

Life is all about relationships. When you pass into eternity, the only thing you take with you is relationships. Being a good steward of relationships first involves your relationship with the Lord and second your relationships with people. Each relationship is unique. Cultivate each relationship according to the distinctiveness of each connection. Relationships are a tremendous responsibility. They take time and work. Good relationships require diligence and thoughtful investment. It is necessary to use discernment regarding relationships. Some relationships are temporary and some are permanent. There are relationships to pursue, and some to leave behind. Some relationships you get little choice over like your biological family. Despite what kind of relationship, the most important ingredient is love and that isn't easy. Relationships with people are extremely difficult when your relationship with the Lord is not what He intended. Jesus told us how there are only two things God wants us to do – love God and love people. The key is that it is impossible to have godly unconditional love for people if you don't love God first. Unconditional love does not mean you accept any behavior. It means that you are not putting conditions on the relationship. Conditions are things like: I'll love you if you get me good gifts, or I'll love you if you don't make me angry. When whatever condition you set isn't met, then love is removed. Unconditional love is not possible in your humanity. It is only through the Lord that you can love without conditions. Unconditional love is a love the Lord wants you to show in your relationships. That means the most important relationship of all is your relationship with the Lord. All other relationships are hinged on that one relationship and it is in that relationship with the Lord that you gain the confidence and discernment to manage all other relationships.

"And you shall love the Lord your God with all your heart, and with all your soul, and with all your mind, and with all your strength... You shall love your neighbor as yourself. There is no other commandment greater than these," Mark 12:30-31 NASB.

"But if anyone does not provide for his relatives, and especially for members of his household, he has denied the faith and is worse than an unbeliever," 1 Timothy 5:8 NASB.

STEWARDSHIP OF OUR PHYSICAL BODIES

You only have your physical body for a short time. It is your responsibility to take care of your body while you live in it. To be a wise steward, you need to take care of yourself first so you can minister and serve others. God instructs you to be a living sacrifice. He asks you to offer your body to Him to use for His purpose and His glory. You are not your own. Remember, EVERYTHING is created by and for God, including you. You are His. The best offering you can give to God is you.

The Bible even breaks it down for you. James instructs you to keep control of your tongue to give honor to God and not hurt others, but to encourage them. Proverbs tells you to watch where your feet go and not to rush into evil, but to carry the gospel to others. There are instructions to keep your eyes from lust, and instead read the Word of God.

Don't forget the practical side of taking care of your physical body. Exercise, manage stress, avoid habit-forming drugs and alcohol, refrain from smoking, drink clean water, breathe pure air, take your vitamins and minerals, and maintain a healthy diet. Being a good steward is a balancing act worth learning to have a long, healthy, happy life. If illness or disease comes knocking at your door, seek the Lord as your Healer. When despair tries to pull you into depression and anxiety, cast it on the Lord and thank Him for the good things. I understand that may seem like a simplistic view of what feels like complicated problems. The point is that the Lord has provided answers to every problem that would try to assault you and your body. As a steward of your body, it is your job to find the answer, declare God's truth, and do the best you can for your temporary shelter. You can bring glory to God by how you steward yourself.

"I will praise You, for I am fearfully and wonderfully made; marvelous are Your works, and that my soul knows very well," Psalm 139:14.

"Do you not know that your body is a temple of the Holy Spirit who is in you, whom you have from God, and that you are not your own? For you have been bought with a price: therefore glorify God in your body," 1 Corinthians 6:19-20 NASB.

"Do not be anxious about anything, but in everything by prayer and supplication with thanksgiving let your requests be made known to God. And the peace of God, which surpasses all understanding, will guard your hearts and your minds in Christ Jesus," Philippians 4:6-7 ESV.

"Casting all your anxieties on him, because he cares for you," Philippians 4:13 ESV.

I'm in Charge of What?

STEWARDSHIP OF THE ENVIRONMENT

God placed the earth and everything in it into Adam's care at the beginning of time. The Lord told Adam in Genesis 1:28 to *"Be fruitful and multiply; fill the earth and subdue it; have dominion over the fish of the sea, over the birds of the air, and over every living thing that moves on the earth."* You, as Adam's child and a servant of Christ, have been called to continue the stewardship of creation. There are three things to remember when considering the environment.

- God created everything. Rocks, dirt, sand, minerals, water, air, plants, fish, mammals, reptiles, amphibians, birds, insects, and so much more. Often, this is simply called nature. Each part of creation has value and depends on other parts of creation and ultimately the motion of nature affects people. For instance, the phosphorous in the dust of the Sahara Desert is vital to the rainforests in the Amazon. How amazing is that?

- God sustains everything. It is God, who makes it rain, grows the grain for food, hangs the stars in the sky, and brings the prey to the predator. There is an order in nature, which is evident in the cycles of life, the seasons, ecosystems, and chemical cycles. God has set the cycles in motion and asks people to respect them and care for them.

- Because of sin and corruption on earth, creation is subject to destruction. God has also set in motion the principle of redemption to be walked out by humankind. Part of humankind's responsibility is to keep your part of the covenant with God by caring for creation and protecting it from the sin and corruption that is loose on earth.

When using and managing the environment, it is important to recognize that your responsibility is to manage and take care of the environment in a way that is not wasteful or destructive and represents the original functions of the environment designed and sustained by the Lord.

"The heaven, even the heavens, are the Lord's: but the earth hath he given to the children of men" Psalm 115:16 NASB.

If you are ever in question about who rules creation, read Job 38 - 41. Job and God were having a conversation. Yes, you can have a conversation with God. Try it! Here is part of what the Lord spoke to Job about who is Master of the universe:

"Then the Lord spoke to Job out of the storm. He said: "Where were you when I laid the earth's foundation? ...Who shut up the sea behind doors when it burst forth from the womb, when I made the clouds its garment ... What is the way to the place where the lightning is dispersed, or the place where the east winds are scattered over the earth? Who cuts a channel for the torrents of rain, and a path for the thunderstorm... Who gives birth to the frost from the heavens when the waters become hard as stone, when the surface of the deep is frozen? Can you bind the chains of the Pleiades? Can you loosen Orion's belt? Can you bring forth the constellations in their seasons or lead out the Bear with its cubs? Do you know the laws of the heavens? Can you set up God's dominion over the earth? ... Do you send the lightning bolts on their way?... Who can tip over the water jars of the heavens when the dust becomes hard and the clods of earth stick together?

It is God and God alone that can do all those things and so much more. He created, sustains, and gives it to you to watch over and enjoy.

Stewardship of Possessions/Money

1 Timothy 6:7 says, ***"For we brought nothing into this world, and it is certain we can carry nothing out."*** You own nothing. Ouch. I know you say you own your house, but do you really? Try not paying your taxes and see how long the government lets you keep your home.

Ownership is an illusion. You have access to some things and use some things. You may have some things in your possession, but none of it is truly yours. You didn't bring it with you when you were born, and you can't take it with you when you die. It might be your responsibility for a while, but it isn't actually yours to own. If it isn't yours, then whose is it? It's God's! Remember that all the earth is the Lord's and everything in it. WHEW! When you get that piece of truth, life is much more restful and peaceful. Stress dissolves when you understand nothing is yours. Matthew 6:25-34 is clear on how you are to view possessions.

"Therefore I say to you, do not worry about your life, what you will eat or what you will drink; nor about your body, what you will put on. Is not life more than food and the body more than clothing? Look at the birds of the air, for they neither sow nor reap nor gather into barns; yet your heavenly Father feeds them. Are you not of more value than they? Which of you by worrying can add one cubit to his stature? So why do you worry about clothing? Consider the lilies of the field, how they grow: they neither toil nor spin; and yet I say to you that even Solomon in all his glory was not arrayed like one of these. Now if God so clothes the grass of the field, which today is, and tomorrow is thrown into the oven, will He not much more clothe you, O you of little faith?

Therefore do not worry, saying, 'What shall we eat?' or 'What shall we drink?' or 'What shall we wear?' For after all these things the Gentiles seek.

For your heavenly Father knows that you need all these things. But seek first the kingdom of God and His righteousness, and all these things shall be added to you. Therefore do not worry about tomorrow, for tomorrow will worry about its own things. Sufficient for the day is its own trouble."

Did you freak out when I said nothing is yours? Don't worry. You can still have things. The truth is that the Lord wants to bless you. He desires to give to you abundantly and watch your joy. Remember the old song and meme: Don't worry, be happy. It may seem trivial and unrealistic, but essentially this is what God is telling you to do. He promises to be your Provider if you will trust Him and keep Him as the top priority in your life. He wants your loyalty and doesn't want you to serve things. He knows what you need and already has it ready for you. He desires that you seek Him first and when you do, **ALL THINGS WILL BE ADDED TO YOU**. All means all. How rich is that? If you have all things, you have no want, no lack, and no deficiencies. That is wealth beyond imagination. Back in the day, it was a common saying in Christian circles that where He leads, He feeds and where He guides, He provides. That is true, but somewhere that became a minimal standard. Christians accepted that God would give enough to just get by. One church I used to attend taught that if you have even one dollar left after paying your bills you were living in abundance That was how I lived for years and it's a very uncomfortable and stressful way to live because it isn't the truth! Jeremiah 29:11 states that God has plans for you and those plans are to prosper you and not to harm you. They are plans to give you hope and a future. Getting by on minimal provision is not hopeful or prosperous. God owns everything, and He wants to share it with you. If you serve the Lord, just ask Him for what you need, desire, and want. He listens and desires to make you happy because He loves you and when you are happy it gives Him great joy.

Kingdom Economics

Kingdom economics is about access. God made everything, and everything is God's. You own nothing, but you have access as a child of God to everything that is God's and that is everything that exists. With that in mind, consider these five practical areas of Kingdom Economics:

- Tithing
- Offering
- Saving
- Investing
- Budgeting

STEWARDSHIP OF THE TITHE

OK, so don't get upset because we are talking about tithing. This is an important part of serving the Lord. The tithe is a barometer that measures trust. It is an opportunity to worship God by showing Him obedience and commitment. The tithe is not something you give God. It's already God's. Remember everything is His already. He just asks that you put some back into the kingdom and you can have all the rest. That's a pretty good deal!

The tithe was instituted as early as Abraham when he gave 10% to the priest Melchizedek. The Old Testament has several scriptures regarding the tithe. In Malachi 3 the Lord reminds His people that He does not change. The tithe is a statement of faith. This hasn't changed, just like God hasn't changed. The tithe is 10% of all your increase. Your increase is your yield. If you plant corn, then your increase is in the corn you harvest. If you work for money, then your increase is your salary or income. Tithing is the practice of giving **10%** of one's income to the Lord. (i.e. If a salary is $2,000.00 per month, the tithe would be $200.00 per month.) Now if you want to sow more than that in the kingdom then do it! The more you sow the more you reap.

Malachi continues by asking, "Will a man rob God?" The people are confused and ask in what way they had robbed God. God's answer is clear, "*In tithes and offerings.*" In this passage, the religious leaders are being addressed. The priests had been diverting the incoming tithe to areas that it should not have been going. God was explaining that because they had deceived themselves into believing what they were doing was okay, they had put themselves under a curse because what they were doing was not okay. God was addressing the issue of their heart not how much they were giving. The tithe isn't about money. It's about your heart. He desires to give to you so abundantly that your blessings overtake you. Your financial commitment to God reflects your level of discipleship, not your pocketbook. Your giving is a statement of faith. Leviticus 27:32 reminds us that the tithe, the tenth one, is holy to the Lord. When you do not tithe you are in fact robbing yourself. God isn't impressed by how much you give. What moves God is the attitude of faith in your heart. God desires to give to you generously and the principle of sowing and reaping works. Generosity attracts more generosity so give freely.

Scriptures promises regarding the tithe:

Increase: *"You shall truly tithe all the increase of your grain that the field produces year by year,"* Deuteronomy 14:22.

Protection & blessing: *"Bring all the tithes into the storehouse, that there may be food in My house, and try Me now in this," Says the Lord of hosts, "If I will not open for you the windows of heaven and pour out for you such blessing that there will not be room enough to receive it. And I will rebuke the devourer for your sakes, so that he will not destroy the fruit of your ground, nor shall the vine fail to bear fruit for you in the field," says the LORD of hosts; "And all nations will call you blessed, for you will be a delightful land," says the LORD of hosts,"* Malachi 3:10-12.

Knowledge and skills: Exodus 35 is full of spiritual blessings, special knowledge, and supernatural skills which are given in response to the obedience of tithing and giving offerings.

The Lord has a purpose for your tithe. The tithe is used to take care of the house of God and its ministers. Leaders of God's house should be paid with honor, so they have time to take care of God's people and minister to the hurting, those with sickness, and the lost. The electric bill and water bill need to be paid at your church's building/s. Do you like heat in winter and air conditioning in summer when you go to church? Do you like running water at the church? What about the single mom who needs food for her kids or the guy who needs gas to get to work but no money to pay it or the elderly couple who can't afford their medicine? How will the church pay bills and help the poor, if you don't do your part? The church depends (or should depend) on the Lord to pay bills and salaries as well as mission work, and the Lord wants to use you to supply that need. **Remember, it isn't your pocketbook God is after, but a committed and fully surrendered heart.**

See the scriptures below.

"Thus you shall also offer a heave offering to the Lord from all your tithes which you receive from the children of Israel, and you shall give the Lord's heave offering from it to Aaron the priest" Numbers 18:28.

"To bring the firstfruits of our dough, our offerings, the fruit from all kinds of trees, the new wine and oil, to the priests, to the storerooms of the house of our God; and to bring the tithes of our land to the Levites, for the Levites should receive the tithes in all our farming communities. And the priest, the descendant of Aaron, shall be with the Levites when the Levites receive tithes; and the Levites shall bring up a tenth of the tithes to the house of our God, to the rooms of the storehouse… And at the same time some were appointed over the rooms of the storehouse for the offerings, the firstfruits, and the tithes, to gather into them from the fields of the cities the portions specified by the Law for the priests and Levites; for Judah rejoiced over the priests and Levites who ministered" Nehemiah 10:37-38, 12:44.

Some teach that the tithe is not a New Testament practice and is no longer something a Christian should do. Jesus does not tell His disciples to tithe. He also does not tell them to stop tithing. The New Testament does demonstrate support for ministers and taking care of the house of the Lord. We learned in the Old Testament that kind of support comes from the tithe. Therefore, the principle of tithing is still viable. If you don't get it and your heart isn't engaged, just be honest with yourself and don't even do it until your heart has the faith to give on this level. Ask the Lord to help you with your faith and start somewhere. Give something and watch God move. I know a man who began giving where his level of faith was. It was a small gift but an honest gift. God began to increase him so he began to give more. The more he gave the more God increased him. At this point in his life, he gives 90% of his income and lives off 10% and his 10% is millions of dollars. Go ahead, give it a try. I guarantee God will show up.

STEWARDSHIP OF THE OFFERING

An offering is all that you give beyond the tithe. The Lord encourages you to give generously and give with joy. *"So let each one give as he purposes in his heart, not grudgingly or of necessity; for God loves a cheerful giver,"* 2 Corinthians 9:7. There are several kinds of offerings. You may hear of different offerings being received at different times in the local church (i.e. Pastoral or love offering, offerings supporting different ministries such as the food pantry, building fund offering). Offerings can also fund works that give glory to God, which may include charities, Christian radio, ministries that have blessed you, and many more. Whatever type of offering you participate in, remember that the Lord is most interested in the attitude of your heart—the attitude of your giving. Exodus 35:21 explains that not only should your giving be cheerful, and offerings should be given willfully. *"And they came, every one whose heart stirred him up, and every one whom his spirit made willing, and they brought the Lord's offering to the work of the tabernacle of the congregation, and for all his service, and for the holy garments,"* KJV.

God has instituted a principle for your giving. *"Give, and it will be given to you: good measure, pressed down, shaken together, and running over will be put into your bosom. For with the same measure that you use, it will be measured back to you,"* Luke 6:38. So give generously and expect to reap what you sowed in abundance.

Many years ago, there was a young mother who was a stay-at-home mom. Her husband did not agree with the principle of tithing. This young mother very much wanted to give to the Lord but had no income of her own and her husband refused to give her money to give. She began giving the church her time, volunteering. She also tithed a few pennies from the grocery money her husband gave her. Little by little things changed. Her children went off to school, and she was suddenly offered a job. Now she had some money to tithe more, which she did faithfully. Soon a different job opportunity materialized and her paycheck doubled. As her tithe kept increasing, so did her opportunities. Now she owns multiple businesses, has several books published, and supports several ministries. God is faithful to His Word.

Stewardship of Saving

The financial principle of saving means you set aside something for future needs. The Lord provides for all your needs, but you have a responsibility to do your part too. The Lord tells you to keep a storehouse. That means save some money. You are not to spend frivolously or irresponsibly. Proverbs tells us, it is a fool who spends all their money and a wise man who prepares. You live in a fallen world, which means life happens. Cars need repairs, roofs leak, kids need new shoes, and doctors want paid. Another reason for saving which often gets overlooked is that you need a vacation. It's ok to rest and have fun, so make some plans and save up for it, then enjoy. Another reason to save is so you have a storehouse available for giving to others. Who knows what opportunity God will bring your way so you can be the one He uses to bless someone in need.

You should always have a thousand dollars tucked away somewhere for emergencies. Practically, you should also have a minimum of three months' salary saved so it is easily accessible if the need arises. A better amount would be a year's salary. Ask God what He thinks is best for you and do it. Those might seem daunting numbers to some. However, it might surprise you how God blesses this principle once you begin to apply it. Put away five dollars each paycheck, and then increase it to ten or twenty as soon as you can. Soon you will be surprised at how much you have saved and you really can have that dream vacation or retire early.

Proverbs 21:20 *"There is treasure to be desired and oil in the dwelling of the wise; but a foolish man spendeth it up"* KJV.

Proverbs 22:3 *"A prudent man foreseeth the evil, and hideth himself: but the simple pass on, and are punished"* KJV.

STEWARDSHIP OF INVESTING

Jesus told a parable in Luke 19 about a nobleman who went away to a far country. There were no planes, trains, or automobiles to make his trip fast so they knew he would be gone for a while. He called ten of his servants and gave them ten minas. A mina is about the equivalent of a quarter of a year's wages. He instructed the servants to "Do business till I come." When he returned, he called the servants to him and demanded an accounting of what they had done while he was away. The nobleman rewarded those who invested and grew their deposit and punished those who hid their deposit. Scripture called the one that did not invest wicked.

The Lord left a deposit with His servants, expecting the deposit to be returned with interest. The principle of investing goes back to Genesis 1 when God gave Adam creation. God told Adam to be fruitful and multiply. Investing follows the principle of multiplication. King Solomon's kingdom grew to be one of the greatest and wealthiest by being fruitful and multiplying. His example of increasing wealth follows some simple steps to successful investing. The first thing Solomon did was ask God for wisdom. Decisions for investing should always start with God. Thinking and planning before investing are important. Many people will promise you get-rich-quick strategies and opportunities to give them money to invest for you. Their promises will sound exciting and tempting. However, it might not be as good a deal as it appears. Get-rich-quick through schemes rarely works. Using knowledgeable and trustworthy advisors will help you invest your money wisely. Though it may seem backward, giving is also an important part of investing. Galatians 6:7 warns you *"Do not be deceived, God is not mocked: for whatsoever a man sows, that he will also reap."* Sowing into other people, families, businesses, or ministries that give God glory can be a very wise investment or place to sow your financial seed. Most of all, be patient and trust God. The same principle applies to the gifts God gives you. Like you invest your financial seed, also grow and invest your spiritual seeds.

In Proverbs 27:23-27, Solomon, who is well known for his wisdom, tells how a good overseer manages assets. In a nutshell, he is saying pay attention and like the nobleman told his servants, "Do business." Jesus is coming back and will take account of what you did with everything He entrusted to you. Be diligent and do business.

"Be diligent to know the state of your flocks, and attend to your herds; for riches are not forever, nor does a crown endure to all generations. When the hay is removed, and the tender grass shows itself, and the herbs of the mountains are gathered in, the lambs will provide your clothing, and the goats the price of a field; you shall have enough goats' milk for your food, for the food of your household, and the nourishment of your maidservants."

STEWARDSHIP OF BUDGETING

Budgeting is about keeping order, maintaining balance, and being stress-free in your finances. When you create and follow a budget, you can see where your money comes from and where it goes. By keeping excellent records, you show you have a financial plan and are being a good steward of the money God gives you. Stewardship isn't about doing things cheaply. It's maintaining order and balance. You can be honest with yourself and avoid financial difficulties. Living without a budget can lead to impulse buying and hasty financial decisions. God desires to bless you abundantly. Your responsibility is to receive it, be thankful, and use it wisely.

Help with budgeting:

1. Budget together as a family. Be honest with one another.

2. List expenses and needs.

3. Prioritize by itemizing expenses including tithe & offering.

4. Learn to say "No!" No Interest! NO! Buy now, pay later! NO! Easy Credit! NO!

5. Seek wise counsel. Just like investing, creating a budget may require help.

"Buy the truth and do not sell it—wisdom, instruction and insight as well," Proverbs 23:23 NIV.

"By wisdom a house is built, and through understanding it is established; through knowledge its rooms are filled with rare and beautiful treasures." Proverbs 24:3 NIV.

Overflow Principle

There is one last thing that is important to know as a Christian steward. When you live as a diligent Christian steward preparing for when the Lord returns, multiplying what He has entrusted to you, and caring for His creation, you put into effect the overflow principle. The definition of overflow is spilling over, running over, crammed full, overloaded, flowing over the edge, filled to the brim, and flowing over. The overflow principle works in all areas – health, spiritual gifts, spiritual fruit, finances and so much more. God loves you so much, He constantly gives to you. He never gives just enough. He presses it down, squishes it into every corner, gives it a good shake so there is not a single spare space, and then pours it out and never stops, so it runs over and over and over. God isn't giving to you just so you can be rich, although that's a nice perk. He gives to you so you can become generous! Check out 2 Corinthians 9:8-15 in the Message Bible:

God can pour on the blessings in astonishing ways so that you're ready for anything and everything, more than just ready to do what needs to be done. As one psalmist puts it,

He throws caution to the winds,

giving to the needy in reckless abandon.

His right-living, right-giving ways

never run out, never wear out.

This most generous God who gives seed to the farmer that becomes bread for your meals is more than extravagant with you. He gives you something you can then give away, which grows into full-formed lives, robust in God, wealthy in every way, so that you can be generous in every way, producing with us great praise to God.

Carrying out this social relief work involves far more than helping meet the bare needs of poor Christians. It also produces abundant and bountiful thanksgivings to God. This relief offering is a prod to live at your very best, showing your gratitude to God by being openly obedient to the plain meaning of the Message of Christ. You show your gratitude through your generous offerings to your needy brothers and sisters, and really toward everyone. Meanwhile, moved by the extravagance of God in your lives, they'll respond by praying for you in passionate intercession for whatever you need. Thank God for this gift, his gift. No language can praise it enough!

You can step into the biblical principle of overflow as you honor the Lord and give freely. So, don't be afraid of the stewardship things we discussed, whether it's time, your gifts, or money. God is generous with all of it. You do your part and His overflow will be a normal way of living for you.

"Give, and it will be given to you: good measure, pressed down, shaken together, and running over will be put into your bosom. For with the same measure that you use, it will be measured back to you," Luke 6:38.

"Honor the Lord with your wealth, with the firstfruits of all your crops; then your barns will be filled to overflowing, and your vats will brim over with new wine," Proverbs 3:9-10 NIV.

"For where your treasure is, there your heart will be also," Matthew 6:21 KJV.

Stepping Stones

1. God made everything, and everything is His.
2. You are a steward of the things God has given you.
3. Be a good steward of time.
4. Give of your abilities and gifts.
5. Protect and grow your relationships.
6. Take care of your physical body.
7. Take care of the environment.
8. Maintain a heart of giving.
9. Follow God's Kingdom economics and prosper.
10. Prepare yourself for overflow—abundance of blessing.

I'm in Charge of What?

WALKING IN STEWARDSHIP

1. Describe the qualities of a Christian steward.

2. To fulfill the call as a good steward of what God has given, you must maintain an attitude of gratitude. Name some things for which you are thankful.

3. There are several areas where you can exhibit good stewardship. Name at least five. In what ways can you improve your stewardship in these areas?

4. Why is tithing important?

5. What steps can you take to increase your finances?

Glossary

SIMPLE GLOSSARY OF A FEW WORDS FROM THE CHRISTIAN FAITH

Adultery - The act of being sexually unfaithful to one's spouse

Agape - Affection, goodwill, love, brotherly love, a love feast

Angel - Messenger of God

Apostasy - Turning away from the religion, faith, or principles that one used to believe

Apostle - One sent forth, one chosen and sent with a special commission as a fully authorized representative of the sender.

Atonement - To cover, blot out, forgive; restore harmony between two individuals.

Attribute – An inherent characteristic

Backslide - To go back to ungodly ways of believing or acting.

Blasphemy - Words or actions showing a lack of respect for God or anything sacred.

Bless - To make or call holy, to ask God's favor, to praise; to make happy.

Blessing - A prayer asking God's favor for something, something that brings joy or comfort.

Born-again – To be begotten or birthed from God, the beginning, to start anew

Carnal - Of the flesh or body, not of the spirit, worldly; seat of one's desires opposed to the spirit of Christ

Cherubim - Guardian angels, angels that guard or protect places

Commitment - A promise, a pledge

Conditional - Placing restrictions, conditions, or provisions to receive

Conversion - Turn, return, turn back; change

Convert - To change from one form or use to another, to change from one belief or religion to another.

Courtship - The act or process of seeking the affection of one with the intent of seeking to win a pledge of marriage

Covenant - A pledge, alliance, agreement

Cult - A body of believers whose doctrine denies the deity of Christ.

Deliverance - A freeing or being freed, rescue; the act of change or transformation.

Demon - Evil spirit

Devil - Principal title for satan, the archenemy of God and man

Dispensation - A period of time, sometimes called ages

Dominion - To rule over, have power over, overcome, exercise lordship over

Eros - Erotic, physical love

Eternal - Existing always, forever, without time

Evangelist - Proclaims the gospel of Jesus Christ

Faith - Believing, trusting, depending, and relying on God

Fellowship - Sharing, communion, partnership, intimacy

Forgiveness - To pardon, release from bondage

Fornication - To act like a harlot, to be unfaithful to God, illicit sexual intercourse

Glorification - Salvation of the body, transforming mortal bodies to eternal bodies

Grace - Unmerited favor of God, help given in the time of need from a loving God

Holy - Set apart, sacred

Intercession - To meet or encounter, to strike upon, to pray for another

Justification - Salvation of the spirit, just as if I never sinned

Marriage - A divine institution designed by God as an intimate union, which is physical, emotional, intellectual, social, and most importantly, spiritual

New Testament - Text of the new covenant

Offering - Everything you give beyond your tithe

Old Testament - Text of the old covenant

Omnipotent - All-encompassing power of God

Omnipresent - Unlimited nature of God, ability to be everywhere at all times

Omniscient - God's power to know all things

Pastor - Shepherds of the body of believers

Philia - Conditional love, based on feelings, friendships

Praise - Thanksgiving, to say good things about, words that show approval.

Prayer - Communication with God

Prophet - One who is a spokesperson for God, one who has seen the message of God and declares that message

Propitiation - To satisfy the anger of God, to gain favor; appease

Rapture - To be carried away, or the catching away of

Reconciliation - Restore harmony or fellowship between individuals, to make friendly again

Redemption - To buy back, to purchase, recover, to Rescue from sin

Regeneration - To give new life or force to, renew, to be restored, to make better, improve or reform, to grow back anew

Repent - To give new life or force, to renew, to be restored, to make better, improve or reform, to grow back a new.

Resurrection - A return to life subsequent to death

Revelation - The act of revealing or making known

Righteousness - Right standing with God, integrity, virtue, purity of life, correctness of thinking

Sacrifice - The act of offering something, giving one thing for the sake of another; a loss of profit

Salvation - Deliverance from any kind of evil whether material or spiritual, being saved from danger or evil; to rescue.

Sanctification - Salvation of the soul. Separation from the seduction of sin

Satan - The chief of fallen spirits, opponent; adversary

Sealing - Something that guarantees, a sign or token, to make with a seal to make it official or genuine

Sin - All unrighteousness, missing the mark, wrong or fault; violation of the law

Spirit - A being that is not of this world, has no flesh or bones

Steward - A guardian or overseer of someone else's property, manager

Supernatural - Departing from what is usual, normal, or natural to give the appearance of transcending the laws of nature

Talent - A natural skill that is unusual.

Tithe - Ten percent of all your increase

Tribulation - Distress, trouble, a pressing together, pressure, affliction

Trinity - Three in one: Father, Son, Holy Spirit

Unconditional - No restrictions, conditions, boundaries, demands, or specific provisions

Will – Choice, inclination, desire, pleasure, command, what one wishes or determines shall be done

About the Author

Pamela is a teacher, mentor, and author of the inspirational book *Destiny Arise* and children's books including *Time in a Tuna*. Pam earned her bachelor's degree at the University of Illinois Springfield, her master's degree in Organizational Leadership at Lincoln Christian University, and her doctorate in Leadership at Christian Leadership University. She serves as a mentor for the Spirit Life Circles sponsored by CLU.

She works from her home in the prairie land of central Illinois. Pam and her bodybuilding husband own a gym/fitness center that promotes living a balanced life. She taught sixth grade for almost twenty years. Pam also taught preschool through adult-age students in various venues. She served as director of Super Church, the children's ministry in the United Methodist Church in her hometown. Pam also served in the church nursery, as director of New Life Ministries Discipleship Program, Vacation Bible School Director, Kingdom Kids Children's Ministry Director, and Sunday School teacher. She has also been on missionary trips. Her favorite trip, so far, was the time she spent in Belize.

Pam enjoys kayaking, bicycling, and riding her motor scooter. When she isn't writing, she enjoys spending time with her four children and their families which includes five grandchildren who are the inspiration of her children's books.

Walking with Jesus Series

Becoming the Best Me I Can Be

Book 1 - There Must Be a Better Way
Walking in Salvation

Book 2 - Lord, I Need Help!
Walking with the Holy Spirit

Book 3 - I Thought I Was Changed
Walking in Transformation

Book 4 - I Am Supernatural
Walking in Spiritual Gifts

Book 5 - I Am Strong
Walking as a Warrior

Book 6 - I Am Fruitful
Walking in the Fruit of the Spirit

Book 7 - Love Letters from God
Walking in the Word

Book 8 - Time in the Garden
Walking in the Power of Prayer

Book 9 - I'm in Charge of What?
Walking in Stewardship

Book 10 - The End of – Well, Pretty Much Everything
Walking into Eternity

Who am I? What am I doing here? Where am I going? Everyone at some point in life asks these questions. You were wired to ask and engineered to pursue the answers. The road to discovering destiny is besieged by fiascoes, failures, and the agony of defeat. If your strength has been depleted and has caused you to give up, sit down, push pause, and snooze until another day, then this book is just for you! Amazing experiences are waiting for you. Get ready to be awakened from the posture of defeat, depression, and despair.

Destiny Arise is an easy-to-read book, providing tools to aid in living an amazing life. This book is designed as a trip adviser for your expedition. It will teach you how to evict the spirit of mediocrity and use your past to propel you into your future. You will learn how to shake off the common, arising to be an uncommon force taking your rightful place in the earth. You can change the world. I pray this book will ignite a passionate fire to pursue your destiny unapologetically. Destiny, awake from your slumber and arise.

www.ingramcontent.com/pod-product-compliance
Lightning Source LLC
Chambersburg PA
CBHW062204100526
44589CB00014B/1949